Lucy AND THE Judge

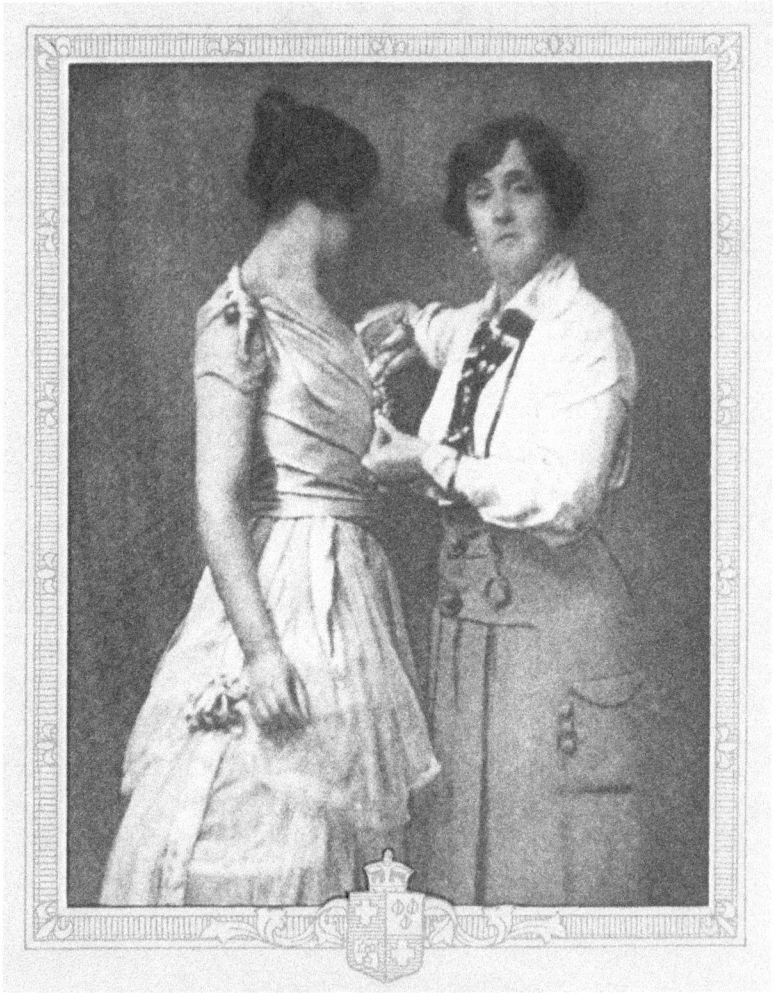

Lady Duff–Gordon at work in her studio

Lucy AND THE Judge

Wood v. *Lucy, Lady Duff-Gordon*

M.H. HOEFLICH **and**
STEPHEN SHEPPARD

TALBOT
PUBLISHING
Clark, New Jersey

TALBOT PUBLISHING

AN IMPRINT OF

THE LAWBOOK EXCHANGE, LTD.

33 Terminal Avenue
Clark, New Jersey 07066-1321

*Please see our website for a selection of our other publications
and fine facsimile reprints of classic works of legal history:*
www.lawbookexchange.com

Library of Congress Cataloging-in-Publication Data

Names: Hoeflich, Michael H., author. | Sheppard, Steve, 1963- author.
Title: Lucy and the judge : Wood v. Lucy, Lady Duff-Gordon / M.H. Hoeflich
    and Stephen Sheppard.
Description: First edition. | Clark, New Jersey : Talbot Publishing, an
    Imprint of The Lawbook Exchange, Ltd., [2022] | Includes bibliographical
    references. | Summary: "A lighthearted review of the historical
    background of and secondary scholarship on the infamous contract case
    Wood v. Lucy, Lady Duff-Gordon"-- Provided by publisher.
Identifiers: LCCN 2022058876 | ISBN 9781616196806 (paperback)
Subjects: LCSH: Wood, Otis F.--Trials, litigation, etc. | Duff Gordon,
    Lucy, Lady--Trials, litigation, etc. | Trials--New York (State) | Breach
    of contracts--New York (State)--Cases. | Fashion design--Law and
    legislation--New York (State)--Cases.
Classification: LCC KF228.W664 H64 2022 | DDC
    346.74702/2--dc23/eng/20230113
LC record available at https://lccn.loc.gov/2022058876

Printed on acid-free paper

Contents

Dear Friends,

A year has passed since the last chapbook appeared in this series, and in that period, my age has increased and my stamina has decreased thanks to a bout with our modern plague. Thus, I sought the assistance of my longtime friend and fellow scholar, Stephen Sheppard, to complete this volume. Because it's been my habit in these volumes to speak in my own voice rather than the neutral voice of the scholar, you will find some passages below in the first person, reflecting my thoughts and experiences over the years. {-MHH} Other sections reflect our shared work. A few, like this greeting, are consciously mixed, with some thoughts of each, separately and others, of both. {-SS} We have added head notes to guide readers and parentheticals of initials to signal changes of voice below. We hope that you will find these more an amusement or a help than a distraction.

Thanks to Greg Talbot and the wonderfully skilled team at his press, Madeleine Johnson and Peter Lo Ricco, you likely received this book in mid-winter. We think that is a fine time for an amusing distraction, and we hope you'll find our gift to be exactly so.

{-MHH and SS}

The Source of our Distraction—

Wood v. Lucy, Lady Duff-Gordon is one of a handful of great cases in the American common law. A public battle between two celebrities of fashion and finance that gave rise to a much-needed reform of contract law, the case also advanced the reputation of a young, ambitious judge of New York's highest court. Judge Cardozo's engagement with this case allowed him to improve the law of contracts and push it toward a more equitable and progressive future, helping to establish consumer protection as a fundamental aspect of commercial law. Today, it stokes the fires of lawyers' and scholars' admiration for Judge Cardozo's creative and radical approach to the law, an approach that made both the case and the judge iconic. Even more than a century later, every American law student begins her career imbibing the creativity and humanity that shines throughout this case in which flawed litigants, through the transformative genius of one of America's greatest judges, continue to influence our law.

A dry, technical summary of the case, which one finds in the hornbooks and the casebooks, would not seem enough to inspire such continuing devotion to the case—nor its influence on the imagination of so many lawyers and legal scholars.

We offer this small book, drawn from the scholarly and literary efforts of so many others who were likewise inspired. Their inspiration—and ours—arose from the story behind the case, which we offer to each of you to enliven your holidays.

As you will see, this is not the product of archival research or deep historical scholarship. It is simply a labor of love that we share with each of you this holiday season. {-MHH and SS}

Introduction

Professor Antony Grafton of Princeton University divided historians into two groups: "parachutists" and "truffle hunters." Parachutists take a broad view of history and human progress; they reap great bounties from their grand narratives. Truffle hunters, on the other hand, take a microscopic, sometimes subatomic, view of historical moments and human events; they are the "micro-historians" whose rewards come not in royalties but in the wee triumphs found by rooting in the weeds of history to unearth small details of past life.[1]

I am most certainly—by temperament and by performance (as evidenced by a career of snuffling for the smallest details of legal history)— a truffle hunter.

I was trained to be a textual scholar but also to be attuned to the artifacts that underlie the texts. One of my favorite courses as a Haverford undergraduate was my senior year historiography seminar, especially the day each of us was handed an object and told to write a research paper identifying the object and placing it in its historical setting.

The objects were chosen to be alien to our historical specializations. I had focused on ancient and medieval history so, of course, my object was a Teotihuacán

---

1 Anthony Grafton, *Bring Out Your Dead: The Past as Revelation* 21-22 (Harvard University Press, 2001); see, also, ibid., in Franceska Trivolato, "Is there a Future for Italian Microhistory in the Age of Global History?," online at https://escholarship.org/content/qt0z94n9hq/qt0z94n9hq_noSplash_99cd35d4d81c295e72aeda0ea85abc24.pdf?t=ncvdkl. This paragraph comes from M.H. Hoeflich & Stephen Sheppard, "The Mystery of the Leavenworth Oaths," forthcoming in the *Kansas Law Review* (2023).

jaguar puppet idol. The two months I spent on that project were sheer joy.

In law school, I was fortunate to have brilliant teachers who taught me to approach each case in varied ways. Guido Calabresi introduced me to the world of economic analysis. Quintin Johnstone and Geoffrey Hazard taught me how lawyers go about their daily tasks, and Grant Gilmore and Jan Deutsch showed me that behind every decision that we read was a narrative of human life, often filled with drama and passion. This last approach was music to my truffle-hunting soul. [*-MHH*]

On Legal Decisions

Legal cases are full of narratives. Witnesses give narratives of their observations. Each party constructs a narrative of facts. Each party creates a doctrinal narrative designed to persuade the court to adopt its reasoning to reach the conclusion it wants. The judge constructs the factual and doctrinal narrative that ultimately speaks for the court.

Lawyers draft most parties' narratives, "cherry-picking" facts from witness observations and tangible evidence to construct the story the lawyers believe will best fit the legal standards and appear most sympathetic to the judge or jury. They similarly elect one among several possible doctrines on which to build the argument that, they hope, most favors their client's cause.

The judge synthesizes these narratives into a decision that amounts to a third narrative. This judicial synthesis selects evidence, facts, and doctrines from the parties' narratives, integrating them into the judge's opinion. The opinion serves several purposes from among a wide range. One of the more likely is to persuade other judges to uphold the opinion on appeal or to apply it later as authority. One of the less likely, oddly, is to serve as an honest record of the judge's intellectual journey—from the first encounter with the dispute between the parties, through the selection among possible reasons to prefer one party's argument over the others, to the decision the judge pronounces in the case.

This complex process is literary as well as legal, as Judge Richard Posner has noted:

> One of the things that judges feel, or should feel, and that the lay public is aware of also, is a series of tensions between various senses of law as form and rule and technique on the one hand, and on the other hand as the rendering of substantial justice. Tensions exist between rule and discretion, between law and justice, between rule and standard, between law and equity, between strict construction and flexible construction, between natural law and positive law, between formalism and realism, and so on. Judges lean toward one end of the spectrum or the other but my own view is that anyone who leans too far either way is a bad judge. Literature can make us—the judges and other members of the legal community—more sensitive to this point.[2]

Judge Posner is, in our experience, absolutely correct. Still, he neglects to mention that in the process of editing narratives to fit the goals present in every case, much evidence of great interest from a human perspective—and quite often from a legal perspective—is never mentioned.[3] The judicial opinions that arise from these cases are often driven by great stories, yet the judges' cool, edited narratives hide the human passions and drama that lie beneath.

The fascination inherent in the "backstory" of law cases has not gone undiscovered in scholarly literature or in teaching.

---

2 Richard A. Posner, "Remarks on Law and Literature," *Loyola University Chicago Law Journal*, Vol. 23, Issue 2, pp. 181-195, 182 (1991).

3 M.H. Hoeflich, "On Reading Cases: The Law Student in Wonderland," *Syracuse Law Review*, Vol. 42, Issue 4, pp. 1163-1188 (1991).

John Noonan, Jr., and Brian Simpson, both masterful scholars and writers, have produced brilliant studies of the stories behind great cases.[4]

We unashamedly here proclaim a well-known, if rarely acknowledged, truth: Doctrine is, in itself, rather boring.

Economic analysis or the subtle dance of precedents may thrill the mathematically obsessed among us. Yet, though they may not admit it, most lawyers and law students find them to be insufficient to arouse the passions. In law school, once one gets beyond the sheer terror of trying to master the material, it is the human stories behind the cases that actually thrill us. We believe that every lawyer and law student comes away from law school with a few favorite cases and, perhaps, a favorite judge. [-*MHH and SS*]

Lucy and the Judge: Two Themes with Countless Variations

For me, that favorite case was and continues to be *Wood* and the favorite judge, Cardozo. This attraction is certainly why one of my first published law review articles—with my mentor, Jan Deutsch—was about Benjamin Nathan Cardozo.[5]

---

4 John Noonan, *The Antelope: The Ordeal of the Recaptured Africans in the Administration of James Monroe and John Quincy Adams* (University of California Press, 1990); A. W. B. Simpson, *Leading Cases in the Common Law* (Clarendon Press, 1995). Two publishers have led significant efforts to expand a genre built on such work, which many of our friends receiving this chapbook will know quite well. Their series not only discovered or promoted these valuable stories but also led many experts in substantive law to discover the inner legal historian. Since 1979, Peter Charles Hoffer, N. E. H. Hull, and William James Hull have edited *Landmark Law Cases and American Society* for The University of Kansas Press, recently releasing Philippa Strum's *On Account of Sex: Ruth Bader Ginsburg and the Making of Gender Equality Law*, their seventy-eighth title. For teaching purposes, Foundation Press's *Law Stories* has twenty-two anthologies collecting one to two dozen histories of leading cases in popular law school subjects, written by scholars and edited by leaders in those fields.

5 J.G. Deutsch & M.H. Hoeflich, "Legal Duty and Judicial Style: The Meaning of Precedent," *St. Louis University Law Review*, Vol. 25, Issue 1, pp. 97-96 (1981).

I am hardly alone in my enduring fascination with *Wood*.[6] The case has the makings of a terrific film: an eccentric aristocratic woman designer, an iconic judge, a New York reporter who could have stepped out of a dime novel, all topped off with a good helping of serendipity. Unsurprising, then, that the case aroused the attentions of generations of scholars, who see in the case all manner of important legal issues.

Dozens of law review articles have been published about the case, including a brilliant piece of legal-historical research by Victor Goldberg and an entire issue of the *Pace Law Review*.[7] Art and culture historians have written about Lucy, Lady Duff-Gordon, who rose to fame as England's first woman couturier.[8] *Titanic* addicts still debate Lucy's and Cosmo's roles in the *RMS Titanic* disaster.[9] And Cardozo, of

---

6 Wood v. Lucy, Lady Duff-Gordon, 222 N.Y. 88, 118 N.E. 214 (N.Y. 1917).

7 Victor P. Goldberg, "Reading *Wood v. Lucy, Lady Duff-Gordon* with Help from the Kewpie Dolls," in —, *Framing Contract Law: An Economic Perspective* (Harvard University Press, 2006); Columbia Law & Economics Working Paper No. 288 (2005). Online at https://scholarship.law.columbia. edu/faculty_scholarship/1393. See the 2008 *Pace Law Review* symposium edition, which is Vol. 28, Issue 2. The introduction to the program is in James J. Fishman, "The Enduring Legacy of Wood v. Lucy, Lady Duff-Gordon," *Pace Law Review*, Vol. 28, Issue 2 (2008). There is more, collected at the end of this tome.

8 The historians are nicely represented by the Victoria & Albert exhibition, "Lucile, Ltd." Basic to all discussions is Lucy's autobiography, *Discretions and Indiscretions* (Frederick A. Stokes, 1932).

9 Recurrent interest is, of course, spurred by every movie about the disaster, which seems to cast increasingly intriguing actors for the Duff-Gordon roles in every outing. Yet events also cause their mid-Atlantic stories to resurface, as when the papers from their legal defense following the evacuation from the ship were found in their solicitor's offices, a century after the fact. See Elizabeth Grice, "Titanic Survivors Vindicated at Last: A Recently Discovered Cache of Letters Seen by The Telegraph Absolves Sir Cosmo and Lady Duff Gordon of Bribery and Cowardice," *The Telegraph*, April 13, 2012, online at https://web.archive.org/web/20120413210622/ http://www.telegraph.co.uk/history/titanic-anniversary/9202821/Titanic-survivors-vindicated-at-last.html.

course, has been written about even more, including books by Judge Posner and by Professors Andrew Kaufman and Richard Pollenberg, among others.[10]

Why, then, do Steve and I send this little chapbook out into the cold wintry air this holiday season? The answer is simple. *Wood* is a marvelous case with wonderful parties and even a bit of mysterious legal doctrine. Most lawyers vaguely remember the case but lack the time or inclination to research the sources or the evolving commentary the case has engendered. Further, unless they delve into the history of women's fashion, they will never see Lucy's dress designs or hear her thoughts about their significance—in her own voice. [*—MHH*]

The Play within the Play: The Facts of the Case

The facts of *Wood* in the reported decision are straightforward, presented in Cardozo's elegant prose:

> The defendant styles herself 'a creator of fashions.' Her favor helps a sale. Manufacturers of dresses, millinery, and like articles are glad to pay for a certificate of her approval. The things which she designs, fabrics, parasols, and what not, have a new value in the public mind when issued in her name.[11]

The remainder of the facts are nothing but a brief description of the contract and of its failure. Yet Cardozo's faint praise for Lucy's capacity to add value to clothes by merely endorsing them is hardly sufficient to explain the nub of the contract itself—how "[h]er favor helps a sale."

---

10 See Richard A. Posner, *Cardozo: A Study in Reputation* (University of Chicago, rev'd ed., 1993), Andrew L. Kaufman, *Cardozo* (Harvard University Press, 1998), and Richard Pollenberg, *The World of Benjamin Cardozo: Personal Values and the Judicial Process* (Harvard University Press, 1997).

11 *Wood* above, p. 90.

The Story Behind the Play within the Play

Lucy, Lady Duff-Gordon was an English celebrity women's clothing designer, with studios in London, New York, and Paris, who conducted her business under the trade name "Lucile." She was known as an innovator in the marketing of women's clothing. She perfected the runway show using live models, animated presentations of her designs artfully raised from the floor on a catwalk through the audience and dramatically lit so that the clothing was inescapably the focus of attention and memory. Her shows were accompanied by carefully arranged music and well-crafted narratives.

The descriptions Lucy crafted to accompany her designs were quite different from anything before them. Each design had a name that evoked a mood, amplified by its narration in a show or its depiction in a display. In her own estimation, one of her greatest achievements was to connect clothing designs to "emotions."[12]

With her fresh designs and effective marketing, Lucy successfully challenged the dominance of the Parisian couturiers on their own turf. And she brought couture designs to the United States, or at least to its elite.

Lucy's innovations went beyond marketing, revising the very concept of women's clothes as both objects and symbols. She had scandalized—but won

---

12 See Valerie D. Mendes & Amy de la Haye, *Lucile Ltd., London, Paris, New York, and Chicago, 1890s-1930s* (V&A, 2009); Randy Bryan Bigham, *Lucile, Her Life By Design: Sex, Style and the Fusion of Theatre and Couture*, p. 192 (Macevie Press Group, 2012).

over—English women by offering them sexy underwear and nightclothes. Her designs freed women from the constricting and often painful corsets and stays that forced their bodies into unhealthy shapes.

Lucy was a true pioneer in fashion design. She mastered the colors of textiles so that she could match a woman's coloring with the color of her fabric. She cut woman's clothes with variety so each woman could have off-the-rack clothes in a bespoke array, so that each lady's selection from the catalog would arrive cut to suit her physical attributes. Lucy's designs were, as her biographer Randy Ryan Bigham aptly claims, "pitch perfect" for the needs and aspirations of the women of the times.[13]

Lucy's fashions swept the English upper class in the early decades of the twentieth century. Her designs—and the sexual and social revolution they helped to create—subtly changed all the tastes of Britain and America in ways beyond their cultural hallmark, the creation of the "IT" girl.[14] Unsurprisingly, Lucy was also a popular costume designer for the theatre productions of London's West End, a perfect outlet for her more flamboyant pieces.

By her own admission, Lucy was not a good businesswoman (although Professor Goldberg disagrees). Her claimed liability served, though, as a fine excuse for her to bring Sir Cosmo

---

13 Above, n. 12.

14 See Meredith Etherington-Smith and Pilcher J. Etherington-Smith, *The "IT" Girls: Lucy, Lady Duff Gordon, the Couturiere Lucile, and Elinor Glyn, Romantic Novelist* (Harcourt, 1987); Hilary A. Hallett, *Inventing the IT Girl: How Elinor Glyn Created the Modern Romance and Conquered Early Hollywood* (Liveright, 2022). Elinor Glyn was Lucy's younger sister.

Duff-Gordon, a minor Scottish aristocrat and Olympic fencer, into Lucile as her business partner. Soon thereafter, they wed; she gained financial benefits along with a new title.[15]

In the first decade of the twentieth century, Lady Duff-Gordon decided to expand her business to the United States. American ladies of the Gilded Age were the perfect audience for her innovative designs, and all went swimmingly for a while. Then, in 1911, Lady Duff-Gordon's fortunes changed. She was accused of tax and customs fraud in the United States. And, far worse, she and Cosmo booked passage on the *Titanic* for its maiden voyage.

Cosmo and Lucy survived the shipwreck, but questions were aired as to their behavior during the tragedy. They were far from the only first-class passengers to find safe seats in a scarce lifeboat, leaving 1,500 others to the sea. Yet someone saw Cosmo, once they were safely about the rescuing *RMS Carpathia*, giving money to the rowers of their lifeboat; thus, the questions. Cosmo was required to testify in London before an official inquiry, and both he and Lucy were subjected to extremely negative treatment in the English press.

---

15 The Duff-Gordon name can be a source of confusion to readers a century later. The confusion derives from the fame of an earlier Lucie, Lady Duff-Gordon, who was Cosmo's mother. Her interests included gruesome criminal trials, heroic soldiers in carnage-rending battles, famous and powerful witches, ancient and modern Egyptians, and anything complicated and German; her disinterests included proximity to her husband, Sir Alexander Cornwall Duff-Gordon, 3rd Baronet of Halkin, who persisted in living in England with its tuberculosis-exacerbating weather. There is no recent biography of Lucie, or her astonishing family, though Lucie's daughter, Janet Ross, wrote the best there is in her edition of Lucie's *Letters from Egypt* (1865, rev'd ed. R. Brimley Johnson, 1902) and her *The Fourth Generation: Reminiscences by Janet Ross* (Constable and Co. 4th ed., 1912). Other than dates and interests, the easy way to distinguish the Ladies Duff-Gordon is that Cosmo's mother's name was abbreviated to "Lucie" with an "i-e," whilst Cosmo's wife spelled the same abbreviation, "Lucy," with a "y".

Cosmo was, eventually, vindicated.[16] Yet by then the public's interest had faded, and the pall on their reputations would persist. The scandal broke Cosmo's spirit and exiled Lucy to her New York outpost. The next few years saw increasing financial challenges for the business, no doubt a result of negative publicity, the psychological effects of the *Titanic* scandal, and changing fashion.

Further, there seems to have been tension between Cosmo and Lucy. Lucy, the person, was under an exclusive contract with Lucile, their company, to design exclusively for Lucile. In exchange, Lucile paid Lucy $200 each week, a not-inconsiderable sum. In spite of this generous compensation, Lucy seems to have chafed under the arrangement—and the control which Cosmo exerted over *her* business.

This stress led Lucy to take several business steps which proved to be extremely unfortunate. First, beginning in 1915, she attempted to market her name and her designs to a broader audience. She succeeded in making endorsement and marketing arrangements with Sears and with Chalmers Motors, and she signed an endorsement contract with a New York promoter and newspaperman, Otis F. Wood. Finally, in 1917 she sold her business to a New York manufacturer. [-*MHH and SS*]

Otis F. Wood

Otis F. Wood was, in his own way, nearly as interesting a character as Lucy, Lady Duff-Gordon. Otis was a grandson of a multi-millionaire newspaper magnate and the son of the notorious Fernando Wood, the Tammany-Hall-sponsored Mayor of New York City, one of the most colorful personalities of his era.

---

16 The letters and statements from the 1912 hearing, which were discovered in the offices of Cosmo's former solicitors a century later, are nicely described and contextualized by livius, at "'Blackguard of the Titanic' Vindicated. Again," The History Blog, April 14, 2012. Online at http://www.thehistoryblog.com/archives/16175.

Otis, but one of Fernando's numerous children, ran an early New York advertising and marketing firm.[17] He became a pioneer in the business of "product placement," the subtle marketing of goods by ensuring the public would just happen to see a branded product in the right place at the right time.

Otis had been involved in a different contractual dispute not long before he sued Lucy. The earlier suit attracted much less public attention, in part because it ended quietly, when Otis lost a pre-trial discovery motion.[18] Yet we take an interest in Otis's early litigation, in part because it was a fight over Kewpie dolls, and in part because Victor Goldberg has shown Otis's fight with Rosie O'Neil, the Kewpies' creator, bears a striking similarity to his suit against Lucy.[19] [-*MHH and SS*]

The Judge

Benjamin Cardozo, one of the greatest of American judges, sat first on the New York Court of Appeals and then on the Supreme Court of the United States. His name is so often invoked as a model jurist that he appears to my students like a man of the status quo. A true judicial radical, he was anything but. Many of Cardozo's decisions boldly changed American private law. His opinions in such cases as *Palsgraf*, *Bloomfield Motors*, *Meinhard*, and *Yellow Cab* changed the course of American tort law, corporate liability, and the law

---

17 Victor Goldberg, *Reading* Wood v. Lucy, cited in full above in note 7.

18 Wood v. Wilson, 167 App. Div. 896, 151 N.Y.S. 853 (N.Y. App., 1ˢᵗ Dep., 1915).

19 Victor Goldberg, *Reading* Wood v. Lucy, cited in full above in note 7. In essence, Wood offered a contract similar to Lucy's to Rose O'Neill Wilson, the creator of the Kewpie doll. Rose was as unsatisfied as Lucy with Wood. Wood sued Rose to enforce their contract, but made such errors in his pleading and discovery that he was tossed out of court. We are all grateful to Victor Goldberg, whose spelunking in the court files fleshes out the bones of an interlocutory appeal on discovery in the appellate division, which is the only easily accessed record in this case.

of fiduciary responsibility. In contract law, the synthesis of his quartet of reform—*De Cicco, Wood, Sun Printing,* and *Allegheny College*—revived the concept of promissory estoppel and transformed it into reliance theory, providing an alternative to the confusing and technical doctrine of consideration.[20] In 1917 he decided both *Wood* and *De Cicco*.[21] In 1923 he decided *Sun Printing*,[22] and in 1927 came his analytic masterpiece, *Allegheny College*.[23]

One of the more interesting aspects of Cardozo's decisions intended to effectuate broad changes in American private law is that they were not cases that stood out as of major importance before Cardozo decided them. Indeed, many of the decisions could easily have been disposed of under existing law; none of them "needed" to be decided as they were, based on novel legal theories.

Thus, the nagging question in my mind for more than forty years: why did he pick them? *De Cicco* was a marriage settlement case with much settled law that could have been used. *Allegheny College* was a charitable donation case for which, again, there was ample precedent. *Sun Printing* was a requirements case in which most observers thought the law was settled. And *Wood* was a case involving the "best efforts"

---

20 See below, nn. 21-23. This sequence of cases was ensconced in Restatement, 1st of Contracts §90 and underlies the examples contained therein.

21 Attilio De Cicco v. Joseph Schweizer et al., 221 N.Y. 431, 117 N.E. 807 (N.Y., 1917) (a parent's promise to his daughter's fiancé to make annual payments to both, if they marry, was enforceable).

22 Sun Printing & Pub. Ass'n v. Remington Paper & Power Co., 235 N.Y. 338, 139 N.E. 470 (N.Y., 1923) (a contract for commercial goods that leaves open both the price and the times for repricing, is inchoate and unenforceable).

23 Allegheny College v. Nat'l Chautauqua County Bank, 246 N.Y. 369, 159 N.E. 173 (N.Y., 1927) (a donor promising a college to fund a scholarship is estopped from ending payments by the college's naming the scholarship for the donor.)

doctrine that could have easily been decided based on existing New York precedent.[24] [*-MHH*]

The Legal Context

Over the course of a decade and through these five principal decisions, Cardozo created an alternative to the confusing and incoherent mess of consideration.[25] The pair of 1917 decisions, *Wood* and *De Cicco*, set the stage for the later, bolder opinions that created an alternative, American jurisprudence of contracts.

We see in the two opinions evidence of Cardozo's search for alternatives to a strict consideration doctrine. *De Cicco* provided an alternative path through a reworking of the doctrine of consideration and the reintroduction of the notions of promissory estoppel and reliance. It was somewhat radical, but, at least, it was rhetorically and conceptually rooted in traditional doctrine.

Wood, on the other hand, departed from traditional doctrine and revived the equitable idea that a set of promises could be legally binding even if the promise to be enforced was technically deficient under traditional contract doctrines.[26] The justification for this move was that the enforceability

---

24 For a contemporary summary by a close observer of Cardozo's contracts opinions during their evolution, see Arthur L. Corbin, "Mr. Justice Cardozo and the Law of Contracts," *Columbia Law Review*, Vol. 39, Issue 1, pp. 56-87, at pp. 60-67; *Harvard Law Review*, Vol. 52, Issue 3, pp. 408-439, at pp. 412-419; *Yale Law Journal*, Vol. 48, Issue 3, pp. 426-547, at pp. 430-437 (1939).

25 See Harlan Fiske Stone, "The "Mutuality" Rule in New York," *Columbia Law Review*, Vol. 16, Issue 6, pp. 443-464 (1916). Cardozo would certainly have read this article very shortly after he received the issue.

26 Indeed, the unanimous appellate division bench, whom Cardozo's opinion reversed, found the contract between Wood and Duff-Gordon lacked consideration and "mutuality" because neither party had made enforceable promises to the other. Wood v. Lucy, Lady Duff-Gordon, 177 App. Div. 624, 164 N.Y.S. 576 (N.Y. App. Div. 1st Dept., 1917).

of the implied promise arose from the fact that the contract at issue was "instinct with an obligation."[27] Mystical as that phrase sounds, its mundane significance is that the plaintiff would not likely have promised the performance required by the agreement unless the defendant had implied the unstated promise in issue.

In each of these decisions, Cardozo offered an untraditional alternative to the expected strict application of consideration theory, which he believed caused serious problems in contract law. [–*MHH and SS*]

---

27 We note that Cardozo did not invent the phrase, which seems to have been first employed by Justice Scott, in the New York Appellate Division, in 1909:

> It is claimed that the contract of employment is unenforceable for lack of mutuality. It is true that plaintiff does not by precise words engage to employ defendant for the term specified, but the whole contract is instinct with such an obligation on its part, and there can be no doubt that upon a fair construction it imports a hiring by the plaintiff, as well as an obligation to serve by defendant.

McCall Co. v. Wright, 133 App. Div. 62, 68, 117 N.Y.S. 775, 779 (App. Div. 1909), aff'd, 198 N.Y. 143, 91 N.E. 516 (1910), though Judge Hiscock neither repeats nor relies on Justice Scott's formula. Cardozo first adapts Justice Scott's aphoristic reasoning in Moran v. Standard Oil Co., 105 N.E. 217, 221 (N.Y. 1914), to interpret an oral agreement. Yet, in *Wood*, the phrase is promoted to serve as the sufficient, modern basis to determine the very existence of a contract.

> The law has outgrown its primitive stage of formalism when the precise word was the sovereign talisman, and every slip was fatal. It takes a broader view today. A promise may be lacking, and yet the whole writing may be 'instinct with an obligation,' imperfectly expressed (Scott, J., in McCall Co. v. Wright, 133 App. Div. 62, 117 N. Y. Supp. 775; Moran v. Standard Oil Co., 211 N. Y. 187, 198, 105 N. E. 217). If that is so, there is a contract.

Wood, 222 N.Y. at 91; 118 N.E. at 214 (1917) (Cardozo, J.).

The Case's Significance

Our purpose in this short volume is not to provide great new insights into the case, the parties, or the judge. Instead, we hope simply to provide the best tidbits from a century's worth of others' writing and research, accompanied by some of the images that lay behind the controversy taken from the Sears 1916 catalogue of Lady Duff-Gordon's designs—with her commentary about them.

Beyond the pure entertainment value of the story, the fascinating characters, and the striking designs, there is also a reason to bring all of this together which might appear to border on the frivolous. Judge Cardozo, along with Justice Holmes, was one of the greatest of judicial stylists. His decisions are models of English prose. The opening line of Judge Cardozo's opinion in this case has fascinated commentators for generations: "the defendant styles herself a 'creator of fashions.'"[28]

There is just a whiff of something negative implied by starting a high-court opinion with a description of a litigant as one who merely "styles" herself in the role by which she is before the court. Granted, the phrase itself came from the defendant's brief to the court, which was in turn taken from marketing materials.[29] Even so, transplanting it to the first line of the court's pronouncement effectively translates it from a term of humility to a term of humbuggery.

Did Judge Cardozo, the retiring man who lived a life as far from the fashionable world as possible, find the idea of fashion—particularly fashion designed by an upper-class English woman who thought a $25 dress was inexpensive enough for a middle-class American woman to purchase—just a bit off-putting?[30] Was he bothered by the notion of a *female*

---

28 Wood v. Lucy, Lady Duff-Gordon, 222 N.Y. at 88, 118 N.E. at 214.

29 See, Professor Goldberg's comments on this point in his article cited n. 7, above.

30 Even unionized workers were unlikely to earn so much in a whole week's

celebrity fashion designer and businesswoman? Or, perhaps it was the designs themselves, which he must have seen if not studied. Did he find them too radical—or too salacious—for his taste? Did he find Lady Duff-Gordon's lengthy and emotive description of each and every design just a bit too much?[31]

Without seeing the designs themselves, we cannot judge. But now, readers, you can see a selection of the designs in this small holiday offering, and you can judge for yourself. [-*MHH and SS*]

Concluding Thoughts

It is difficult to reconstruct Cardozo's thinking as to why he chose to use *Wood v. Lucy, Lady Duff-Gordon* to experiment with ways to expand contract doctrine and offer an alternative to traditional consideration theory. But, we might suggest here, perhaps, that serendipity played a role.

First, Cardozo would have wanted the cases in which he was trying to change contract law to be read by as many lawyers and others as possible. The involvement of Lucy, Lady Duff-Gordon and Otis F. Wood as the litigants would certainly have made an otherwise humdrum contracts dispute newsworthy. Both parties were celebrities and, to some degree, not only famous but notorious. How many cases could Cardozo hope to find before him with such newsworthy litigants?

Second, Cardozo had a family connection to Wood. Cardozo's father Albert, before he was forced off the bench, had decided an earlier case involving Wood's father. Might

---

work. With the exception of a few engineering positions, most work on a union scale in 1916 was $20 or less for a six-day work week. See Bureau of Labor Statistics, Bulletin of the United States Bureau of Labor Statistics, No. 245, *Union Scale of Wages and Hours of Labor, May 15, 1917*. Of course, non-unionized work usually paid much less.

31 Professor Monroe Freedman accuses Judge Cardozo of abusing Lucy in his opinion; see, M. Freedman, "Cardozo's Opinion in Lady Lucy's Case: "Formative Unconscionability," Impracticality and Judicial Abuse," in the 2008 *Pace Law Review* symposium edition, cited, n.7, above, p. 404.

this serendipitous fact have inclined him to help Wood in the case before him and (unless such a result would have clearly thwarted the law or reached an unjust result) find in his favor?

As you might suspect, we leave such judgments to you.

We are neither clothing designers nor fashion historians, so our remarks on Lady Duff-Gordon's design creations will be minimal. As is our Neo-Socratic way, we leave you to judge her designs and her design philosophy from her own statements in the Sears catalogue, reprinted later in this book.

Nevertheless, we will make several statements that we consider worth making:

Lucy became the first successful English woman designer in what had been a male-dominated world. It is no accident that Lucy's designs moved away from the stifling, restricting, and uncomfortable designs of her male predecessors and contemporaries and thereby became immensely popular with her women customers.

Equally, her appeals to emotion and palette were simply beyond the imagination of her male competitors. And, above all, Lucy wanted her customers to be beautiful and sexy, something quite radical for her era.

Lucy, Lady Duff-Gordon was a creative genius who revolutionized western fashion. And Benjamin Nathan Cardozo was a judge who revolutionized American law. That the two not only encountered each other in this case, but that the case became an icon of the American legal canon is a fact, in itself, worthy of wonder. [-*MHH and SS*]

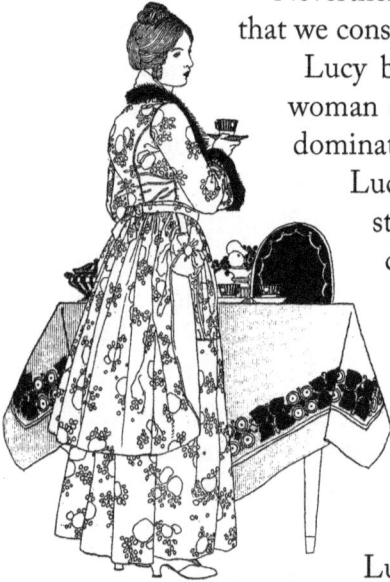

Holiday Wishes from Michael,

In the prior chapbook in this series, I suggested readers might want to sit in a comfortable reading chair before a warming fire, glass of port in one hand, and read the antiquarian extracts contained therein. This year, I suggest a slightly different setting to enjoy the present work.

I hope you might read this after a splendid Christmas feast, the table laid with the best silver and china, and the diners dressed in their finest holiday clothes.

From Steve,

It might suit your circumstances to read this wee book a few days before or after your holiday feast. Whenever you do, please invite a friend or relative to join you. It is always more fun and more memorable to read when you share what you read with people you enjoy.

And From Us Both

Then, perhaps, may you raise a glass to toast the memories of Lucy, Lady Duff-Gordon, of Otis T. Wood, and, of course, of Judge Benjamin Cardozo.

Suggestions for Further Reading[32]

Judge Cardozo

Cardozo, Benjamin. *Law is Justice: Notable Opinions of Mr. Justice Cardozo* (A.L. Sainer, ed.) (Lawbook Exchange, 2014).

Kaufman, Andrew L. *Cardozo* (Harvard University Press, 1998).

Polenberg, Richard. *The World of Benjamin Cardozo: Personal Values and the Judicial Process* (Harvard University Press, 1997).

Posner, Richard A. *Cardozo: A Study in Reputation* (University of Chicago Press, rev'd ed., 1993).

The Duff-Gordons

Lucy

Arlen, Tessa. *A Dress of Violet Taffeta* (Berkley/Penguin, 2022) [a fictionalized account of Lucy's life and career].

Aspinwall, Grace. "Lady Duff-Gordon: A Titled Designer of Clothes Who Aims to Dress the Soul," *Good Housekeeping* (Nov. 1910), at 572-573.

Bigham, Randy Bryan. *Lucile, Her Life by Design: Sex, Style and the Fusion of Theatre and Couture* (Macevie Press Group, 2012).

Etherington-Smith, Meredith & Pilcher J. Etherington-Smith. *The "IT" Girls: Lucy, Lady Duff Gordon, the Couturière Lucile, and Elinor Glyn, Romantic Novelist* (Harcourt, 1987).

---

32 We wish to acknowledge the work of Roman Panickar, KU Law '24 in assisting in the compilation of this bibliography.

Hallett, Hilary A. *Inventing the IT Girl: How Elinor Glyn Created the Modern Romance and Conquered Early Hollywood* (Liveright, 2022).

Lucy, Lady Duff-Gordon. *Discretions and Indiscretions* (Frederick A. Stokes, 1932).

Mendes, Valerie D. & Amy de la Haye. *Lucile Ltd: London, Paris, New York and Chicago, 1890s–1930s* (V&A, 2009).

Mower, Sarah. "A Scandal Survives: The Story of Fashion Designer (and Titanic Passenger) Lucile," *Vogue* (Apr. 13, 2012), https://www.vogue.com/article/a-scandal-survives-the-story-of-fashion-designer-and-titanic-passenger-lucile [https://perma.cc/G86K-UBMU].

Schweitzer, Marlis. "Patriotic Acts of Consumption: Lucile (Lady Duff Gordon) and the Vaudeville Fashion Show Craze," *Theatre Journal* Vol. 60, Issue 4, pp. 585-608 (2008).

Sidell, Misty White. "The birth of the designer collaboration: Meet the couturier whose 1916 line for Sears sparked a modern fashion phenomenon," *Daily Mail* (Sept. 18, 2013), https://www.dailymail.co.uk/femail/article-2424054/Designer-collaboration-Lady-Lucile-Duff-Gordons-1916-line-Sears-sparked-modern-fashion-phenomenon.html [https://perma.cc/J3GR-UZ79].

"Society: At Lady Duff-Gordon's Chansons Vivantes, Worthy Cause Wrought Exquisite Effect," *Vogue* (Apr. 1, 1916), at 54-55.

Totzke, Thorsten. *Portfolio of Titanic's Lady Duff-Gordon's Original Designs* (Thorsten Totzke, 2019).

Cosmo

Grice, Elizabeth. "Titanic Survivors Vindicated at Last: A Recently Discovered Cache of Letters Seen by The Telegraph Absolves Sir Cosmo and Lady Duff Gordon of Bribery and Cowardice," *The Telegraph* (Apr. 13, 2012), https://web.archive.org/web/20120413210622/http://www.telegraph.co.uk/history/titanic-anniversary/9202821/Titanic-survivors-vindicated-at-last.html [https://perma.cc/E2YE-37AT].

Lucie

Frank, Katherine. *Lucie Duff Gordon: A Passage to Egypt* (Tauris Parke, 2007).

Lucie, Lady Duff-Gordon. *Letters from Egypt* (1865, rev'd ed. R. Brimley Johnson, 1902).

Ross, Janet. *The Fourth Generation: Reminiscences by Janet Ross* (Constable and Co., 4th ed., 1912).

The Cases

Allegheny College v. Nat'l Chautauqua County Bank, 246 N.Y. 369, 159 N.E. 173 (N.Y., 1927).

Attilio De Cicco v. Joseph Schweizer et al., 221 N.Y. 431, 117 N.E. 807 (N.Y., 1917).

Sun Printing & Pub. Ass'n v. Remington Paper & Power Co., 235 N.Y. 338, 139 N.E. 470 (N.Y., 1923).

Otis F. Wood v. Lucy, Lady Duff-Gordon, 222 N.Y. 88, 118 N.E. 214 (N.Y., 1917).

The Commentators

Deutsch, J.G. & M.H. Hoeflich. "Legal Duty and Judicial Style: The Meaning of Precedent," *St. Louis University Law Review*, Vol. 25, Issue 1, pp. 97-96 (1981).

Goldberg, Victor P. "Reading *Wood v. Lucy, Lady Duff-Gordon* with Help from the Kewpie Dolls," *Columbia Law and Economics Working Paper No. 288* (2005). https://papers.ssrn.com/sol3/papers.cfm?abstract_id=870474 [https://perma.cc/DVH6-8G3C].

Hoeflich, M.H. "On Reading Cases: The Law Student in Wonderland," *Syracuse Law Review*, Vol. 42, Issue 4, pp. 1163-1188 (1991).

Noonan, John. *The Antelope: The Ordeal of the Recaptured Africans in the Administration of James Monroe and John Quincy Adams* (University of California Press, 1990).

Posner, Richard A. "Remarks on Law and Literature," *Loyola University Chicago Law Journal*, Vol. 23, Issue 2, pp. 181-195, 182 (1991).

Pratt, Walter F. Jr. "American Contract Law at the Turn of the Century," *South Carolina Law Review*, Vol. 39, Issue 2, pp. 415-464 (1988).

Pace Law Review. *Symposium: The Enduring Legacy of Wood v. Lucy, Lady Duff-Gordon*, Vol. 28, Issue 2 (2008).

Simpson, A.W.B. *Leading Cases in the Common Law* (Clarendon Press, 1995).

Otis F. Wood, Plaintiff,

v.

Lucy, Lady Duff-Gordon, Defendant

Amended Complaint, Read in Support of Motion
Supreme Court, New York County

Plaintiff, above named, appearing by his attorney,
John J. Rooney, complaining of the defendant,
and for an amended complaint, alleges:

First: That on or about the 1st day of April,
1915, the plaintiff herein entered into a contract
in writing with the defendant herein, wherein
and whereby it was agreed, as follows:

"Whereas, the said Lucy, Lady Duff-Gordon, occupies a
unique and high position as a creator of fashions in America,
England and France,

"And whereas, her personal approval and endorsement
over her own name of certain articles and fabrics used not only
in the manufacture of dresses, millinery and other adjuncts of
fashion, but also divers other articles of use to people of taste has
a distinct monetary value to the manufacturers of such articles,

"And whereas, the said Otis F. Wood possesses a business
organization adapted to the placing of such endorsements as
the said Lucy, Lady Duff-Gordon, has approved,

"It is agreed by the said Lucy, Lady Duff-Gordon, that
the said Otis F. Wood is hereby granted the exclusive right
to place such endorsements on such terms and conditions as
may in his judgment, and also in the judgment of the said
Lucy, Lady Duff-Gordon, or A. Merritt, her personal business
adviser, be most advantageous to the said Lucy, Lady Duff-
Gordon, and the said Otis F. Wood.

"AND WHEREAS, the said Lucy, Lady Duff-Gordon's approval and selection of certain articles and fabrics used in the manufacture of her model gowns, millinery and other adjuncts of fashion which she designs, has a distinct monetary value to the manufacturers of such articles used,

"IT IS AGREED, that the said Otis F. Wood shall have the exclusive right to make such terms under the same conditions as set forth in this agreement, but it is expressly understood and agreed by both parties that no such arrangement can be entered into before such goods have been personally passed upon and approved by the said Lucy, Lady Duff-Gordon, and also that nothing in this limits the right of the said Lucy, Lady Duff-Gordon, to select and use any fabrics or other articles whatsoever in her business, provided the said Lucy, Lady Duff-Gordon, does not allow her endorsement to be used for said goods.

"AND WHEREAS, the said Lucy, Lady Duff-Gordon, creates from time to time different articles, such as parasols, belts, handbags, garters, etc., etc., and these also have a distinct monetary value independent of their own specific use in her own dress creations sold at her own houses of 'Lucile,'

"IT IS AGREED, that the said Otis F. Wood shall have the exclusive right of placing these articles on sale or licensing the rights to others to manufacture and market such articles.

"IT IS EXPRESSLY UNDERSTOOD AND AGREED by both parties that nothing in this agreement shall apply to any other executed or pending contract made by the said Lucy, Lady Duff-Gordon, prior to this date, nor does this agreement include any rights to moving pictures, theatrical performances and lectures, the distribution of photographs of her gowns or publication of signed articles by the said Lucy, Lady Duff-Gordon, or any articles or books which may be hereafter written by her, or the sale of portraits of dresses unless said permission be expressly granted by the said Lucy, Lady Duff-Gordon, or by the said A.

Merritt, from time to time, as such permission may be asked by the said Otis F. Wood.

"It is AGREED, that in the event any arrangement is made with the third party running longer than the time stated in this agreement, that the said Otis F. Wood is to share in the returns from same during his lifetime of such agreement, and the said Otis F. Wood's rights thereunder are not to cease at the expiration of this agreement.

"It is UNDERSTOOD, that the Fashion Portfolio Service, suggested by the said Otis F. Wood, is covered under the terms of this agreement.

"It is AGREED, that all profits and revenues derived under any contracts made with third persons hereunder are to be paid over and collected by the said Otis F. Wood, and that all said profits and royalties are to be divided equally between the parties hereto, it being expressly understood, however, that the cost of securing such profits and royalties shall be directed toward this half share of Otis F. Wood, the said Lucy, Lady Duff-Gordon, receiving a full half share of all said profits and royalties without any expense whatsoever being directed against it; and it is further expressly understood that the said Otis F. Wood shall account monthly, to wit, on the first day of every month, to the said Lucy, Lady Duff-Gordon, for all such moneys received by him. The said Otis F. Wood agrees to take out and procure such patents, copyrights or trade-marks as may in his judgment be necessary to protect such names, ideas or articles as are affected hereby and to carry out such actions or proceedings as may, in his judgment, be necessary in order to protect such patents, copyrights or trade-marks. And it is further understood that such patents, copyrights or trade-marks shall be held in the name of the said Lucy, Lady Duff-Gordon, and that the expense of obtaining such patents, copyrights or trade-marks and of protecting the same from infringement, shall be shared equally by the parties hereto. But it is expressly understood and agreed that no such suit or action can be begun by the said Otis F. Wood without the consent of the said Lucy, Lady Duff-Gordon, or of the said A. Merritt.

"IT IS AGREED, that this contract shall cover a period of one year from the signing hereof, and that at the expiration of the said period it shall automatically renew itself for another year, and thereafter from year to year, unless either party shall give notice in writing to the other party of his or her intention to terminate this agreement not less than ninety (90) days preceding the expiration of the said term of one year or the expiration of any succeeding term thereafter."

Otis F. Wood, Appellant,

v.

Lucy, Lady Duff-Gordon, Respondent

Court of Appeals of New York
Argued November 14, 1917
Decided December 4, 1917

Opinion of the Court

Cardozo, J.

The defendant styles herself "a creator of fashions." Her favor helps a sale. Manufacturers of dresses, millinery and like articles are glad to pay for a certificate of her approval. The things which she designs, fabrics, parasols and what not, have a new value in the public mind when issued in her name. She employed the plaintiff to help her to turn this vogue into money. He was to have the exclusive right, subject always to her approval, to place her indorsements on the designs of others. He was also to have the exclusive right to place her own designs on sale, or to license others to market them. In return, she was to have one-half of "all profits and revenues" derived from any contracts he might make. The exclusive right was to last at least one year from April 1, 1915, and thereafter from year to year unless terminated by notice of ninety days. The plaintiff says that he kept the contract on his part, and that the defendant broke it. She placed her indorsement on fabrics, dresses and millinery without his knowledge, and withheld the profits. He sues her for the damages, and the case comes here on demurrer.

The agreement of employment is signed by both parties. It has a wealth of recitals. The defendant insists, however, that it lacks the elements of a contract. She says that the plaintiff does not bind himself to anything. It is true that he does not promise in so many words that he will use reasonable efforts to place the defendant's indorsements and market her designs. We think, however, that such a promise is fairly to be implied. The law has outgrown its primitive stage of formalism when the precise word was the sovereign talisman, and every slip was fatal. It takes a broader view to-day. A promise may be lacking, and yet the whole writing may be "instinct with an obligation," imperfectly expressed (SCOTT, J., in *McCall Co.* v. *Wright*, 133 App. Div. 62; *Moran* v. *Standard Oil Co.*, 211 N. Y. 187, 198). If that is so, there is a contract.

The implication of a promise here finds support in many circumstances. The defendant gave an *exclusive* privilege. She was to have no right for at least a year to place her own indorsements or market her own designs except through the agency of the plaintiff. The acceptance of the exclusive agency was an assumption of its duties (*Phœnix Hermetic Co.* v. *Filtrine Mfg. Co.*, 164 App. Div. 424; *W. G. Taylor Co.* v. *Bannerman*, 120 Wis. 189; *Mueller* v. *Bethesda Mineral Spring Co.*, 88 Mich. 390). We are not to suppose that one party was to be placed at the mercy of the other (*Hearn* v. *Stevens & Bro.*, 111 App. Div. 101, 106; *Russell* v. *Allerton*, 108 N. Y. 288). Many other terms of the agreement point the same way. We are told at the outset by way of recital that "the said Otis F. Wood possesses a business organization adapted to the placing of such indorsements as the said Lucy, Lady Duff-Gordon has approved." The implication is that the plaintiff's business organization will be used for the purpose for which it is adapted. But the terms of the defendant's compensation are even more significant. Her sole compensation for the grant of an exclusive agency is to be one-half of all the profits resulting from the plaintiff's efforts. Unless he gave his efforts, she could never get anything. Without an implied promise, the transaction cannot have such business "efficacy as both parties must have intended that at all events it should have" (BOWEN, L. J., in *The Moorcock*, 14 P.

D. 64, 68). But the contract does not stop there. The plaintiff goes on to promise that he will account monthly for all moneys received by him, and that he will take out all such patents and copyrights and trademarks as may in his judgment be necessary to protect the rights and articles affected by the agreement. It is true, of course, as the Appellate Division has said, that if he was under no duty to try to market designs or to place certificates of indorsement, his promise to account for profits or take out copyrights would be valueless. But in determining the intention of the parties, the promise *has* a value. It helps to enforce the conclusion that the plaintiff *had* some duties. His promise to pay the defendant one-half of the profits and revenues resulting from the exclusive agency and to render accounts monthly, was a promise to use reasonable efforts to bring profits and revenues into existence. For this conclusion, the authorities are ample (*Wilson* v. *Mechanical Orguinette Co.*, 170 N. Y. 542; *Phœnix Hermetic Co.* v. *Filtrine Mfg. Co.*, *supra*; *Jacquin* v. *Boutard*, 89 Hun, 437; 157 N. Y. 686; *Moran* v. *Standard Oil Co.*, *supra*; *City of N. Y.* v. *Paoli*, 202 N. Y. 18; *M'Intyre* v. *Belcher*, 14 C. B. [N. S.] 654; *Devonald* v. *Rosser &* *Sons*, 1906, 2 K. B. 728; *W. G. Taylor Co.* v. *Bannerman, supra*; *Mueller* v. *Bethesda Mineral Spring Co.*, *supra*; *Baker Transfer Co.* v. *Merchants' R. & I. Mfg. Co.*, 1 App. Div. 507).

The judgment of the Appellate Division should be reversed, and the order of the Special Term affirmed, with costs in the Appellate Division and in this court.

Cuddeback, McLaughlin and Andrews, JJ., concur; Hiscock, Ch. J., Chase and Crane, JJ., dissent.

Judgment reversed, etc.

PORTFOLIO
of Lady Duff-Gordon's
ORIGINAL DESIGNS

SEARS, ROEBUCK AND CO.

DISTRIBUTORS OF

WOMEN'S WEARING APPAREL

DESIGNED BY LADY DUFF-GORDON

FOR THE WOMEN OF AMERICA

Fall & Winter
1916-1917

CHICAGO

HOMAN AVENUE AT ARTHINGTON STREET

FIFTH AVENUE AT 19TH STREET

NEW YORK

THIS GARMENT *is one of my own designs. I hope very much that it may harmonize perfectly with your individuality as we had planned to have it. That is what it should do. My models are designed for that effect. And I am so anxious to have you know that I am interested, personally, in your dress problems. I want you to write me, as your friend, about them. Please bear in mind that the arrangement I have with* SEARS, ROEBUCK AND CO. *carries with it the assurance of their absolute guarantee of satisfaction to you. If you buy one of my models and it does not suit you in every particular, you may send it back for exchange to their Chicago Office. Or, it may be returned and your money will be refunded without question.*

Lady Duff Gordon

115 FIFTH AVENUE
NEW YORK

A CARD like the one shown here, carrying the personal guarantee of Lady Duff-Gordon, is sent with every garment in this Style Book. In addition, the garments carry also Lady Duff-Gordon's personal label, stitched in the lining or band. We are very happy to co-operate in this guarantee in the most unqualified manner and to assure the women of America that we will not consider any transaction closed until the purchaser of a Lady Duff-Gordon garment is completely satisfied.

SEARS, ROEBUCK AND CO., CHICAGO.

Page Three

"LET'S GO A-VISITING"

Morning or afternoon dress of French serge. Made in navy blue or golden brown. Lady Duff-Gordon model No. 31A75½. PRICE *$20*

This dress would cost $518.28 if purchased in October 2022.

SEARS, ROEBUCK AND CO.
Distributors of
LADY DUFF-GORDON MODELS

"Let's Go A-Visiting"

JUST a little visit to a friend or two all on a pleasant forenoon—this little morning dress suggests such pleasing occupations. It is simple enough to be perfectly correct for morning wear and handsome enough to do honor to any occasion.

The quiet tones of the brown or blue serge in which this is made are relieved by the vest and collar of white silk and the odd plaid cuffs and collar facing. Everything about this design is trim and tidy, and the daintiness of the waist is emphasized by the narrow leather belt. The long, drooping shoulders ending in the sleeve puff are quaint and unusual, and the fullness of the skirt is placed in quite a different way than common.

The style of the back is as fetching as the front of this model, so you can be sure of the admiring comments that follow, as well as those that greet you in this frock. The pleats both back and front are narrow, carrying out the straight lines of the design, and should be kept neatly pressed down all the time.

A rather plain, simple hat should be worn with this little visiting dress, and high boots, preferably with patent leather vamps and cloth tops.

This is a frock you will wear times without number when you want to go "a-visiting," because you will know you appear very smart and well dressed in it. It is especially good on slender figures.

Lucy Duff Gordon

MODEL NO. 31A75½

Morning or afternoon dress of French serge in navy blue or golden brown. White silk vest and collar. Misses' sizes, 14, 16, 18 and 20 years. Women's sizes, 32 to 44 inches bust measure. It will take from twelve to fifteen days to make this model after your order is received. In ordering be sure to give model number and color.

MODEL No. 31A75½
Delivery charges prepaid by us. PRICE $20

See Page 48 for Measuring Directions

THIS GARMENT is sold with our unconditional guarantee. If your purchase is not entirely satisfactory in every detail, it will be exchanged to please you without charge. Or, if you prefer, your money will be refunded without question. The personal guarantee of Lady Duff-Gordon, as shown on page 3 of this Style Book, accompanies each garment in addition to ours.

SEARS, ROEBUCK AND CO.

BACK VIEW OF MODEL No. 31A75½

Page Twenty-Five

It represented, on average, one week of union wages in 1916.

"MY PROMISE"

Afternoon frock of charmeuse and crepe Georgette.   Made in all black, all white, or old China blue.   Lady Duff-Gordon model No. 31A10½.   PRICE *$27*⁵⁰

This frock would cost $712.64 if purchased in October 2022.

SEARS, ROEBUCK AND CO.
Distributors of
LADY DUFF-GORDON MODELS

"My Promise"

*T*HERE is sincerity and truth and wholesomeness in the charm this model conveys, which makes me want to show it to you personally and let you see how well it becomes you. It is dainty, without being flimsy or perishable. "My Promise," together with "The Curate," would almost make a complete wardrobe for any woman. In that case, of course, it should be in all black or all white, though it is a little gem in old China blue, if you have several afternoon frocks so that you can change about.

The skirt is very full, and is slightly stiffened about half-way up. A tiny frill of lace peeps below the lower edge and the row of small buttons gives the needed decorative touch.

The bodice is softly draped and gathered into the trim, fitted girdle. The sleeves are very long and full, with a cluster of dainty pin tucks. They slip low down off the shoulders and give a graceful droopy look, quite fascinating. There is a little standing collar at the back which is always becoming. "My Promise" may be worn as correctly by young girls as by mature women, and in either case, it will give no end of pleasure. Of course, it is better on slight than stout figures.

Lucile Duff Gordon

MODEL No. 31A10½

Afternoon dress of charmeuse and Georgette crepe in all white, all black or old China blue. Misses' sizes, 14, 16, 18 and 20 years. Women's sizes, 32 to 44 inches bust measure. It will take from twelve to fifteen days to make this model after your order is received. In ordering be sure to give model number and color.

MODEL No. 31A10½
Delivery charges prepaid by us.   PRICE **$27**50
See Page 48 for Measuring Directions

THIS GARMENT is sold with our unconditional guarantee. If your purchase is not entirely satisfactory in every detail, it will be exchanged to please you without charge. Or, if you prefer, your money will be refunded without question. The personal guarantee of Lady Duff-Gordon, as shown on page 3 of this Style Book, accompanies each garment in addition to ours.

SEARS, ROEBUCK AND CO.

BACK VIEW OF
MODEL No. 31A10½

Page Nine

It represented more than a week of union wages in 1916.

"MY DREAM GIRL."

Evening gown of taffeta silk in pink, light blue, maize or orchid. Lady Duff-Gordon model No. 31A40½.   PRICE *$32*

This gown would cost $829.25 if purchased in October 2022.

"My Dream Girl"

WHEN I was designing this model, I had in my mind a picture of the bright eyes, red lips and flushed cheeks that go with youthful happiness. I could see this girlish figure appearing among her young friends in lovely unconsciousness of her charm, yet all the time making a fascinating picture in her dainty frock, so perfectly suited to her individuality.

"My Dream Girl" is made in softest shades of silk taffeta with beautiful lace outlining sleeves and corsage, and the point of the fitted bodice. Filmy chiffon covers the neck and shoulders and a band of silk ribbon follows the edge of the V-neck and peeps from under the lace cascades. The full skirt has just a suggestion of draping on the lower edge at each side. The graceful panniers are faced with soft satin of a darker shade, and caught up with perky little bows. A light hoop holds the skirt out over the hips.

This is a very girlish model to be worn only by the girl-woman standing "where the brook and river meet." "My Dream Girl" is very lovely made up in shades of pink, light blue, maize or the exquisite orchid tints, with touches of contrasting color. A little French corsage bouquet of vari-colored flowers completes the picture.

Lucile Duff Gordon

MODEL. NO. 31A40½

Taffeta evening gown furnished in pink, light blue, maize and orchid. Made only in misses' sizes 14, 16, 18 and 20 years. It will take from twelve to fifteen days to make this model after your order is received. In ordering be sure to give model number and color.

MODEL No. 31A40½
Delivery charges prepaid by us.   PRICE **$32**

See Page 48 for Measuring Directions

THIS GARMENT is sold with our unconditional guarantee. If your purchase is not entirely satisfactory in every detail, it will be exchanged to please you free of charge. Or, if you prefer, your money will be refunded without question. This personal guarantee of Lady Duff-Gordon, as shown on page 3 of this Style Book, accompanies each garment in addition to ours.   SEARS, ROEBUCK AND CO.

BACK VIEW OF
MODEL No. 31A40½

It represented more than a week and a half of union wages in 1916.

"THE INVITATION"

Street costume of all-wool cheviot trimmed with Krimmer fur. Made in light gray, black or navy blue. Lady Duff-Gordon model No. 31A65½. PRICE $37.50

This ensemble would cost $971.78 if purchased in October 2022.

SEARS, ROEBUCK AND CO.
Distributors of
LADY DUFF-GORDON MODELS

"The Invitation"

DON'T you want to come along? She's running away for a bit of an outing, so pink cheeks will grow pinker and bright eyes brighter. This cozy street costume seems to invite you out for a walk just to show how stunning your companion looks. There's a piquant charm about the fuzzy new ruff, over which the eyes peer most alluringly, and it's a strong-minded man or woman who can say "No" to this fascinating "Invitation."

This costume is made for frosty days, in warm cheviot, and whether it is in light gray or navy blue or black, the gray Krimmer fur gives a lovely,

youthful touch and makes this a striking model. The double cape over the shoulders is very modish, as you can see, and gives more warmth, too, where it is most needed.

The skirt is extremely plain and simple, of a style that anyone can wear, with just a panel front and back and pockets at either side. There's a quality that we call "dash" about this model and, withal, it is a perfectly correct street costume of the most approved type.

"The Invitation" is suitable for all ages, but the coat is a bit too full over the hips for any but slim figures.

Lucy Duff Gordon

MODEL No. 31A65½

All-wool cheviot street costume in light gray, black or navy blue, silk lined and trimmed with gray Krimmer fur. Misses' sizes, 14, 16, 18 and 20 years. Women's sizes, 32 to 42 inches bust measure. It will take from twelve to fifteen days to make this model after your order is received. In ordering be sure to give model number and color.

MODEL No. 31A65½
Delivery charges prepaid by us. PRICE $37.50

See Page 48 for Measuring Directions

THIS GARMENT is sold with our unconditional guarantee. If your purchase is not entirely satisfactory in every detail, it will be exchanged to please you without charge. Or, if you prefer, your money will be refunded without question. The personal guarantee of Lady Duff-Gordon, as shown on page 3 of this Style Book, accompanies each garment in addition to ours. SEARS, ROEBUCK AND CO.

Page Twenty-Three

BACK VIEW OF MODEL No. 31A65½

It represented more than a week and a half of union wages in 1916.

"JOY IS CALLING"

Evening gown of cream embroidered net with pink, blue or Nile green ribbons and drop skirt. Lady Duff-Gordon model No. 31A25$\frac{1}{4}$.   PRICE *$44*

This gown would cost $1,140.22 if purchased in October 2022.

SEARS, ROEBUCK AND CO.
Distributors of
LADY DUFF-GORDON MODELS

"Joy Is Calling"

*C*OME out and be the playmate of joy!" This is the message my fancy read into this dainty design, made to be worn on joyous occasions.

This is a truly party frock with all the delightful frills and fluffiness that real parties demand. It is made of cream net, richly embroidered, combined with ribbon and satin, in wild-rose pink, spray blue, or Nile green. The skirt has deep, frilly flounces with bands and festoons of the ribbon hemstitched in with glinting silver thread. The fitted bodice shows a quaint coat effect in the front, which hangs in graceful fullness below the waist all around. A deep satin girdle defines the waist, finished with ribbon bows and a softly shaded French corsage bouquet. The skirt is held out with a light hoop. The drop skirt of charmeuse matches the ribbons and is flounced with lace. Stockings and slippers may be the same shade as the ribbons or they may be cream color to match the net.

The age of the one who wears my "Joy is Calling" frock is of little importance. It is quite as fitting for mature years as for youth. The color of the ribbon should be chosen with a bit of care, though the quantities of lace about the neck and shoulders make a lovely soft setting for any face.

I am sending this design out to you with the wish that you may have many a happy evening wearing it.

Lucile Duff Gordon

MODEL No. 31A25½

Embroidered net with pink, blue or Nile green ribbons and drop skirt to match. Made in misses' sizes 14, 16, 18 and 20 years and women's sizes 32 to 44 inches bust measure. It will take from twelve to fifteen days to make this model after your order is received. In ordering be sure to give model number and color.

MODEL No. 31A25½
Delivery charges prepaid by us. PRICE $44

See Page 48 for Measuring Directions

THIS GARMENT is sold with our unconditional guarantee. If your purchase is not entirely satisfactory in every detail, it will be exchanged to please you free of charge. Or, if you prefer, your money will be refunded without question. The personal guarantee of Lady Duff-Gordon, as shown on page 3 of this Style Book, accompanies each garment in addition to ours. SEARS, ROEBUCK AND CO.

BACK VIEW OF MODEL No. 31A25½

Page Forty-Three

It represented more than two weeks of union wages in 1916.

53

"DOUCHKA"

Evening wrap of velveteen. Made in black, sapphire blue or rose, trimmed with fur. Lady Duff-Gordon model No. 31A100½.　　PRICE $45

This wrap would cost $1,166.13 if purchased in October 2022.

It represented more than two weeks of union wages in 1916.

How to Order from
Lady Duff-Gordon's Style Book

SHOPPING by mail is becoming recognized by women of judgment as the most convenient, the most comfortable method of buying merchandise of every kind. It means just the pleasant task of looking at pictures, then writing your order down, which is much simpler than buying in a store can ever be. Of course, there is a best way to write your orders, a way which means quickest and surest delivery. If you follow the suggestions given here, you will come to like this plan of buying better than any other way of shopping.

After you have looked over the illustrations in this Style Book and decided which of these models you want, then write your order and be sure to give us the information asked for below.

FIRST: Write down the model number (as shown opposite illustration) and color you have selected from those listed for that model.

SECOND: Your height, your weight and your age.

THIRD: *Your measurements*, and these should be taken very carefully according to the instructions given here.

Chest measurement—Measure all around body close under the arms and well up over the shoulder blades at back. Tape should meet in front above the bust and directly across the chest.

Bust measurement—Measure all around body, same as for chest measure, *except*, tape must meet in front directly across fullest part of bust.

Sleeve length—Measure from armhole along inside

seam of sleeve to wrist or where sleeves are short to length desired.

Length of waist in back—Measure from collar seam straight down back to waistline.

Waist measurement—Measure around the smallest part of waist.

Hip measurement—Measure all around body 6½ inches below smallest part of waist.

Front length of skirt—Measure from smallest part of waist down front to length of skirt desired.

Side length of skirt }
Back length of skirt } To be taken same as above.

FOURTH: State how you want goods shipped— Parcel Post, or Express.

SPECIAL SIZES not specified on the previous pages will be made up at an extra charge of 10 per cent.

FINALLY AND MOST IMPORTANT

Send your full name and address carefully and legibly written as follows:

Name_____City or Town_____

R. F. D., P. O. Box or Street No._____State_____

If your shipping point is different from your Post Office address, please give name of shipping point, as well as county, state and name of express company. If shipment is to be made to another party, instead of yourself, write other party's full name and address clearly.

HOW TO SEND MONEY. The best way is Post Office Money Order, Express Money Order, Bank Draft or Check. *Do not send coin.* We prepay express or postage to your home on all Lady Duff-Gordon garments.

IMPORTANT. When you have put into your order all the information we ask for, take the following list and check the questions over with your order, to be sure that nothing has been omitted.

Questions to be answered	Measurements	
Name and Address	Chest	Front length of skirt
Model number	Bust	Side length of skirt
Color wanted	Sleeve length	Back length of skirt
Height	Length of waist in back	*Shipping instructions*
Weight	Waist measurement	Parcel Post
Age	Hip measurement	Express

If all this information is correctly given, it will avoid delay and insure greater satisfaction with your purchase.

Remember that our unconditional guarantee accompanies every garment in this Style Book. If your purchase is not entirely satisfactory in every particular, it will be exchanged to please you. Or, if you prefer, it may be returned and your money will be refunded

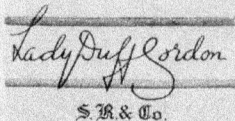

without question. Lady Duff-Gordon's personal guarantee (as reproduced on page 3 of this book) goes with these models in addition to ours. Also the "Lady Duff-Gordon" label, which is her personal signature woven in silk, is stitched into the lining or band of each of these garments and no Lady Duff-Gordon model goes out without it. SEARS, ROEBUCK AND CO.